Make a New Friend in Jes

PassAlong Arch® Books
Jesus with friends close to
children all around the worl
When you've enjoyed thi
along to a friend. When you
ished, mail this book to the address below. Concordia Gospel Outreach promises to deliver your book to a boy or girl somewhere in the world to help him or her learn about Jesus.

Myself

My name ______________________

My address ______________________

____

My PassAlong Friend

My name ______________________

My address ______________________

____

When you're ready to give your PassAlong Arch® Book to a new friend who doesn't know about Jesus, mail it to

Concordia Gospel Outreach 3547 Indiana Avenue St. Louis, MO 63118

PassAlong Arch Books

59-1461	God's Easter Plan
59-1462	Jesus Stills the Storm
59-1463	God's Good Creation
59-1464	Noah's Floating Zoo
59-1469	Baby Moses' River Ride
59-1470	Jonah's Fishy Adventure
59-1471	Baby Jesus, Prince of Peace
59-1472	Jesus' Big Picnic
59-1477	Daniel in the Dangerous Den
59-1478	Moses and the Freedom Flight
59-1479	Jesus and Jairus' Little Girl
59-1480	Peter and the Biggest Birthday
59-1481	Jesus and the Little Children
59-1482	Jesus and the Grumpy Little Man
59-1483	David and the Dreadful Giant
59-1484	Journey to the Promised Land

3558 S. Jefferson Avenue, St. Louis, MO 63118-3968
Manufactured in the United States of America

5 6 7 8 9 10 03 02 01 00 99 98 97

God's Easter Plan

John 20:1–18 for Children

By Carol Greene
Illustrated by Michelle Dorenkamp

CPH®
SAINT LOUIS

reary, weary was the world
On that first Christmas, when
God sent His Son to earth to bring
Us back to Him again.

That Christmas baby, Jesus, grew,
And when He was a man,
He taught the world God's loving ways.
He showed God's loving plan.

"Plan?
What plan?"

But some folks did not feel God's love,
In spite of all He'd done.
They made an angry, hateful plan
To kill God's only Son.

They nailed poor Jesus to a cross
And left Him there to die.
Oh, dreary, weary was the world
And thunder shook the sky.

"How could they *do* that to Jesus?"

Nearby a group of women stood.
They watched until the end.
And one was Mary Magdalene.
He'd been her dearest Friend.

Then men put Jesus in a tomb,
And Mary said, "It's done."
But God's plan wasn't finished yet.
God's plan had just begun.

Then Mary Magdalene went home
And one long night crept by,
And one long day. It seemed as if
All Mary did was cry.

But as the second night grew short
And Sunday morn drew near,
Mary sat up in her bed.
"I can't, I *won't* stay here."

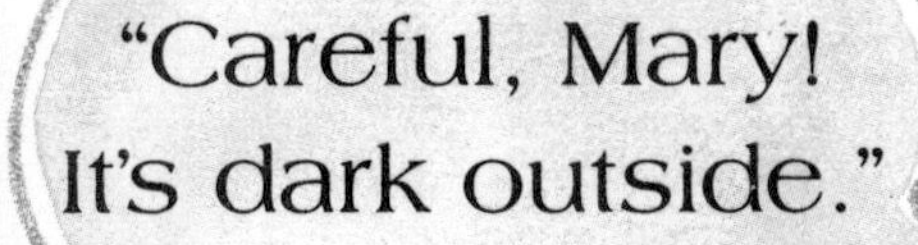
"Careful, Mary!
It's dark outside."

His tomb is in a garden. Yes,
I'm sure I know the way
I'll sit there very quietly
And think of Him and pray."

But when she got there, Mary found
The tomb was open wide.
Her Lord, her Jesus, wasn't there.
"They took Him!" Mary cried.

I'll tell His other friends," she thought,
As through the streets she flew.
"I'll wake up John and Peter first.
They might know what to do."

When John and Peter heard the news,
They stared at her, then ran.
And Mary panted, far behind.
They all forgot God's plan.

John ran fastest. He was first
To peek into the tomb.
Just some cloths that Jesus wore
Lay in the little room.

Up came Peter and the two
Stepped carefully inside.
And then John thought, and then he knew,
Why their Lord Jesus died.

We didn't understand," said John,
"What Jesus meant back then.
He said He'd die to save the world,
Then come alive again.

"He's living, Peter! We are saved
And God's plan has come true.
We'll be God's children always now
It's what He came to do."

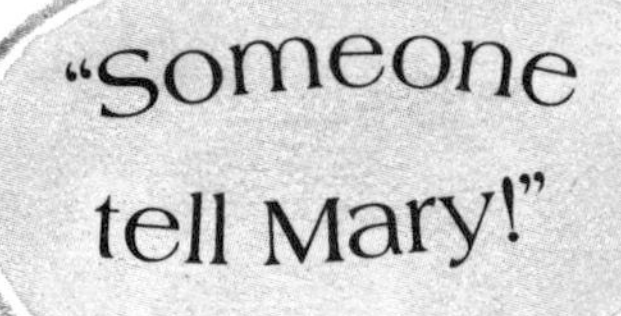

Off they rushed, those joyful men,
With news they had to share.
They ran right past poor Mary, who
Was standing, weeping, there.

Flowers danced and dewdrops sang
From every leaf and stone.
But dreary, weary was her world
And she felt so alone.

Then Mary looked into the tomb,
Too sad to be afraid,
And saw two angels sitting where
Her dearest Friend was laid.

"Why do you weep?" the angels asked.
And she could barely say,
"My Lord is gone, my Lord is gone.
They've taken Him away."

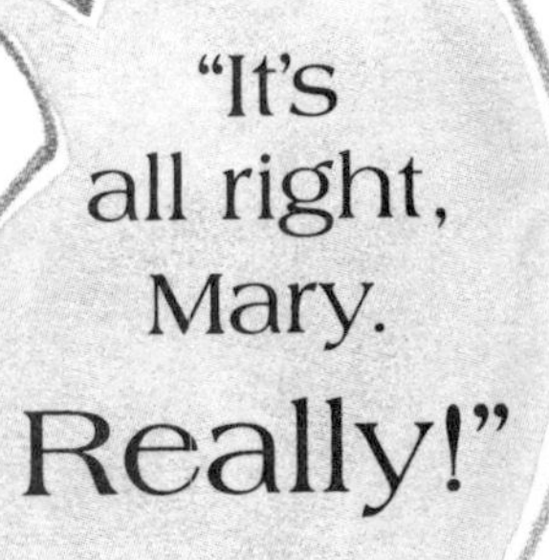
"It's all right, Mary. Really!"

And Mary turned around again
Into the garden's light.
Someone stood there, Mary knew.
But tears had dimmed her sight.

"Why the weeping?" asked a voice.
"Who are you looking for?"
"Are you the gardener? Tell me where
My Lord is, if you are."

"Maybe the gardener will tell Mary."

That gentle voice, so full of love,
Spoke to her once again.
"Mary!" said her risen Lord.
And Mary knew Him then.

Teacher!" Mary cried and reached
To touch Him. But He said,
"I must go to My Father. Tell
My other friends instead.

"I'm going to My Father. He's
Your Father, too, you know.
He's My God and He's your God.
Tell the others, Mary. Go!"